QUOTES I:I

Charleston, SC
www.PalmettoPublishing.com

Quotes 1:1
Copyright © 2024 by Sanjna S Katyal

All rights reserved
No portion of this book may be reproduced, stored in a retrieval system, or transmitted in any form by any means–electronic, mechanical, photocopy, recording, or other–except for brief quotations in printed reviews, without prior permission of the author.

First Edition

Paperback ISBN: 979-8-8229-3970-7

QUOTES 1:1

Written by Sanjna S Katyal

Co-Authored by Aayush Katyal
and Sarthak Katyal

**Dedicated to my uncles
R.N Sehgal and Dr.A Nijhawan.**

You held our hand,
And made us Stand.
You made us laugh aloud,
Taught us to respect all in the crowd.
To be humble and grateful,
To learn with books and always be truthful.
Special you always will be to us forever,
You might be far, but in my heart, you live ever and ever.

Acknowledgements

I am grateful to the crystal-clear innocence of my sons who were the propeller in the creation of Quotes 1:1. This journey has been fruitful and thought provoking because it involved engaging ourselves in simple moments that matter the utmost that makes them indispensable.

Table Of Contents

Motivation 1

Courage 2

Happiness 3

Hope 4

Author's Note

Quotes 1:1 is an ocean of thoughts over the waves of reason and emotions shared between a mother and her son when she was driving him to School every morning.

It's an innocent conversation about the everyday chaos of life that helped both of them to lighten up, to laugh together, to relax, while discussing simple school events. It reinforces an amicable bond of parental joy that helped build a castle of dreams on bricks of hope and relief.

It is the carving on the canvas of life, that glitters with simple things that matter to create an everyday impact. It sets the stage of self-awareness anchored with happiness, hope, courage and motivation. An echo reminding us to enjoy today at its best.

Quotes1:1 is for you and for me, let us cherish happiness in every moment we see!

MOTIVATION

It's all in the mind, where half the Battle is won and half the Battle is lost.

Today is a great day, but I can make it better.

If I walk into a room and saw everyone I ever knew, I would want to find myself cause, I lost that guy a long time ago!

Tomorrow unfolds, what I carve today.

Add the happiness, subtract the worry, multiply the hard work and divide the fear, the equation is called life.

COURAGE

If you knew my story you would wonder; how I haven't given up and how I still smile.

Fight your fears, or your fears will fight you.

Life is like concrete; it's rough, but it's up to you, if you want to pave it out.

Play the game don't let the game play you.

Self-doubt is the first and the final hurdle.

HAPPINESS

"Who says with age you get boring?"

My happiness is my own recipe in the making.

Your focus is the measure of the truth, in your will to perform.

Happiness is the ever blooming blossom that does-not await any season.

Happiness is the soul of life.

HOPE

I found my Smile in the same place I lost it.

Faith is the anchor for Hope.

It takes Light, to lighten the Darkness.

Be the horizon where the Sun never sets.

Hope is the symphony of life, that applauds every moment.

About The Author

Sanjna S. Katyal is a Managing Partner at InSearch Global Consulting.

Quotes 1:1 is reflective of her personalized moments with her sons **Aayush Katyal**, a junior in Morris Catholic High School, and **Sarthak Katyal** a junior in University of Illinois Urbana-Champaign.

It is an encouraging journey shared between them that has helped enlighten the parental bond of self-realization. It is an insight into the everyday moments that sometimes inspire but other times make you perspire. It is an innocent journey to understand the thoughts that define ones happiness.

It helps co-relate her own childhood which is a paradise of joy. Above all, it is a stage of self-awakening in everyday battlefield of life; wherein success and failure, happiness and sorrow, are like melodies composed together to sing along.

www.ingramcontent.com/pod-product-compliance
Lightning Source LLC
LaVergne TN
LVHW021241080526
838199LV00088B/5447